THE PICK OF

Furry Logic

10
TEN SPEED PRESS
Berkeley | Toronto

Jane Seabrook

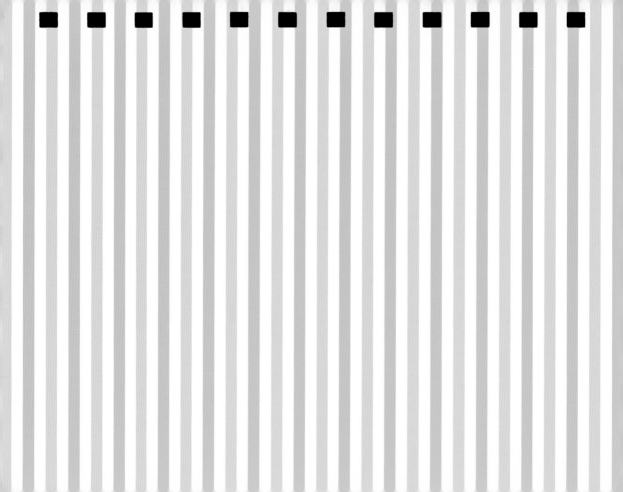

THE PICK OF

Furry Logic

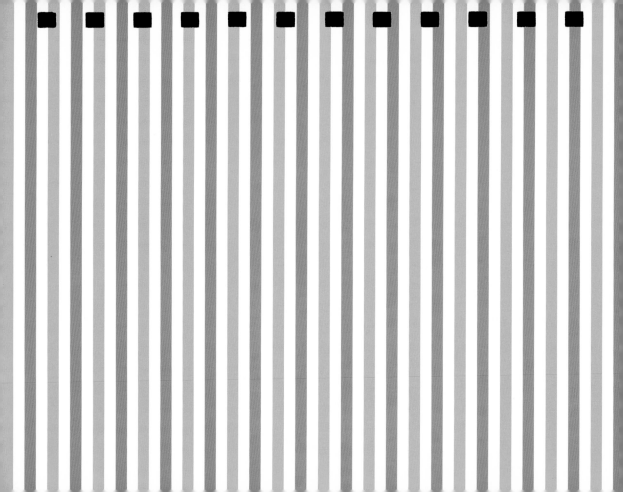

Smile first thing in the morning.

Get it over with.

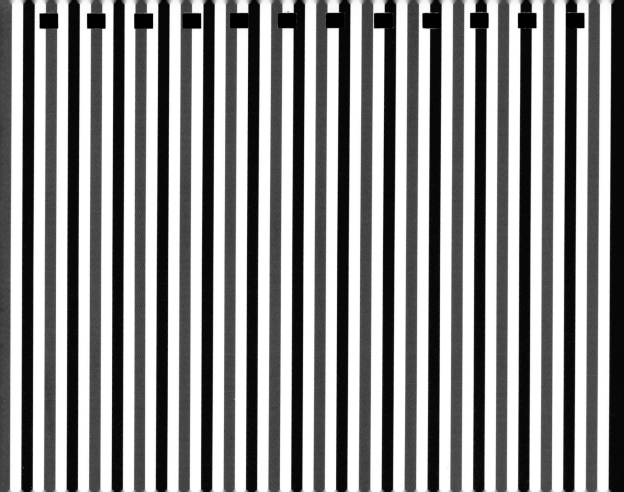

Those are my principles,

and if you don't

like them . . .

well, I have others.

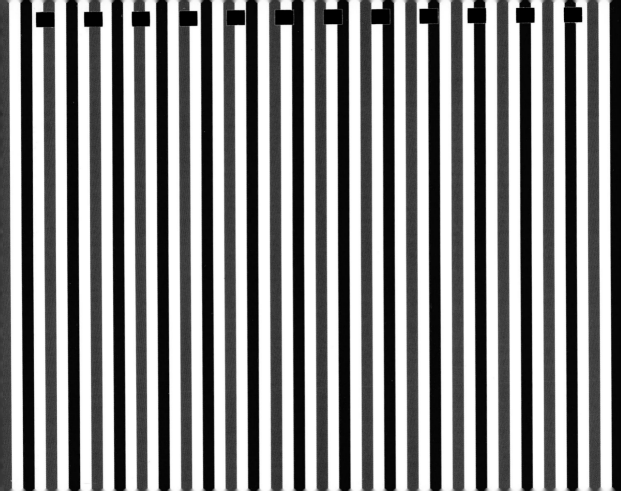

All power corrupts.

Absolute power

is kinda neat.

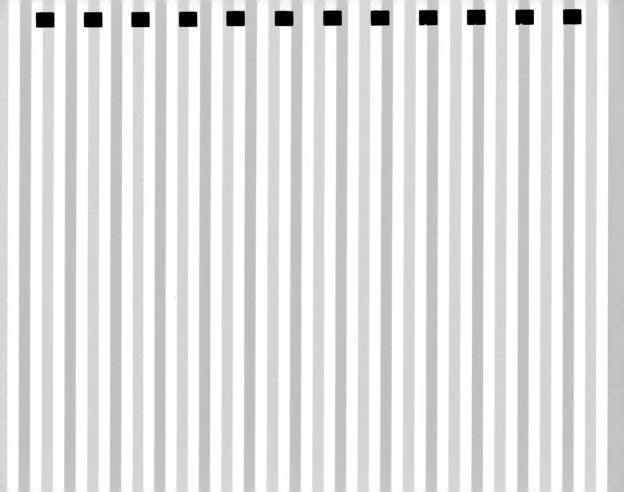

The trouble

with work

is it's

so daily.

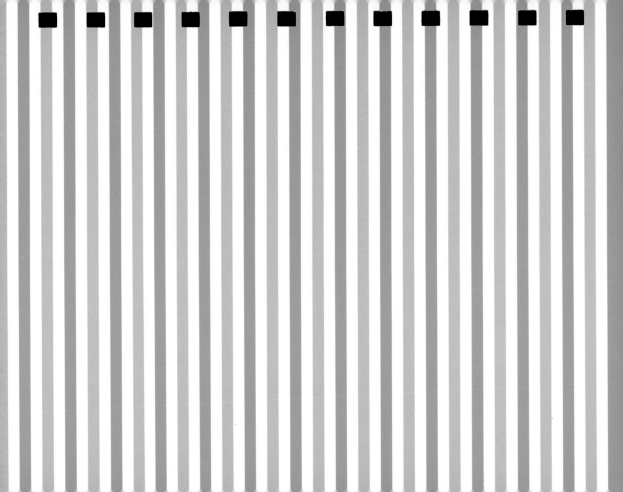

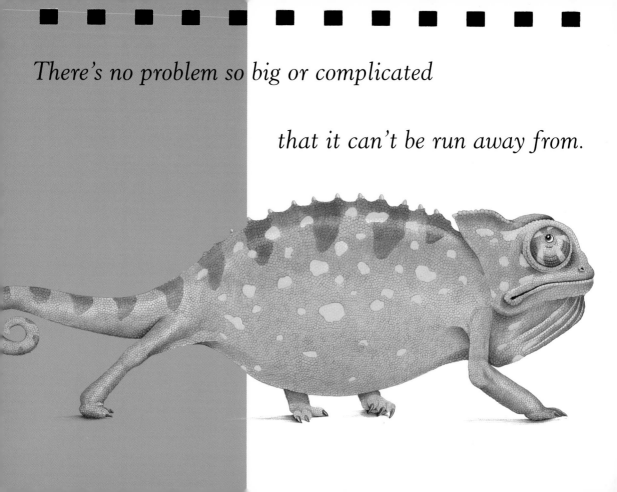

There's no problem so big or complicated

that it can't be run away from.

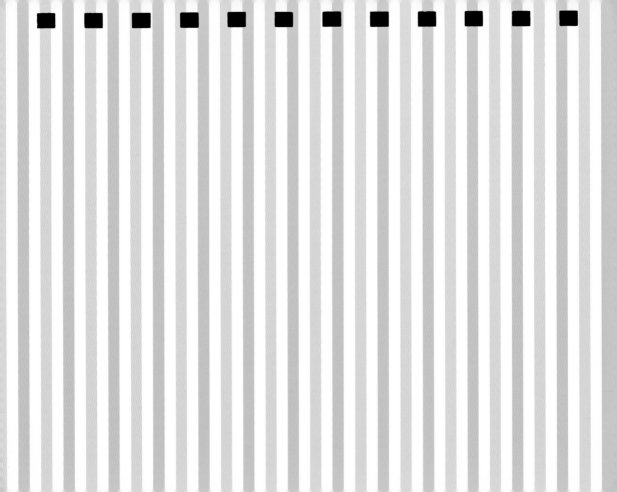

I always try to go

the extra mile at work,

but my boss always finds me and brings me back.

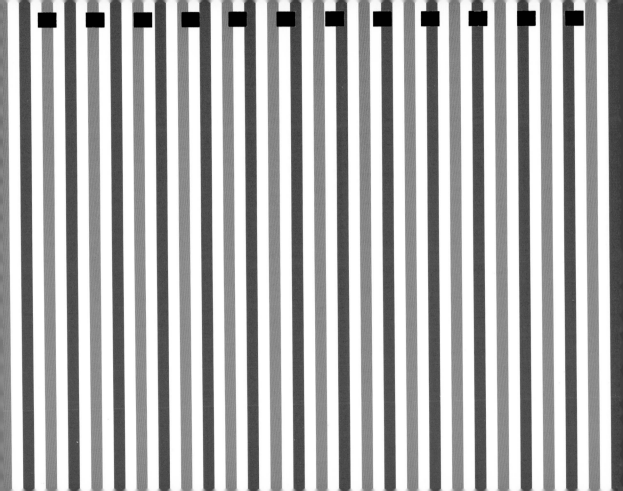

I would be unstoppable. If I could just get started.

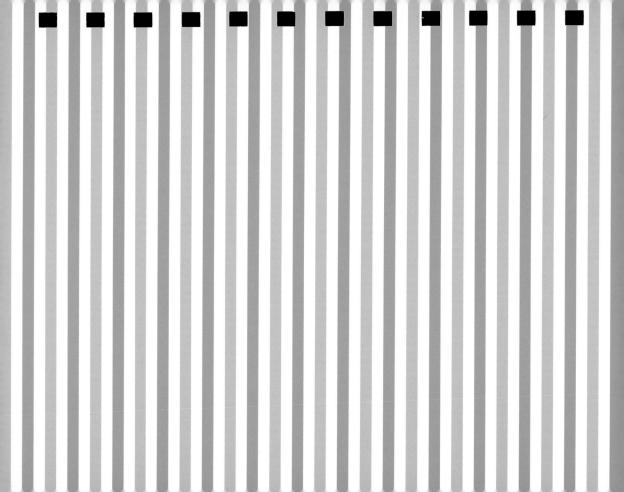

Life is

full of challenge

and frustration.

But sooner or later

you'll find the

hairstyle you like.

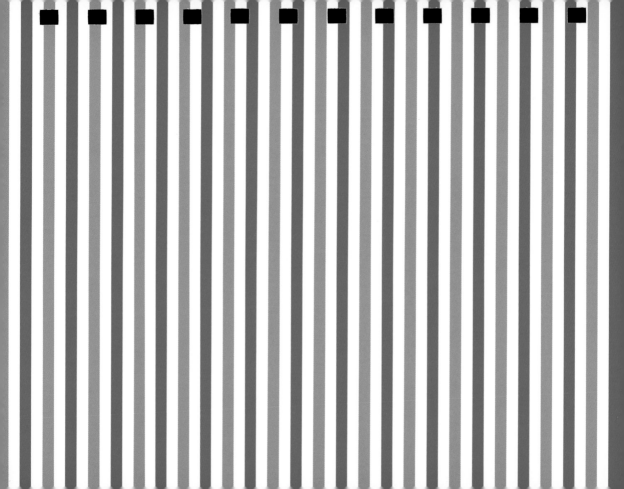

Be yourself.

Nobody is

better

qualified.

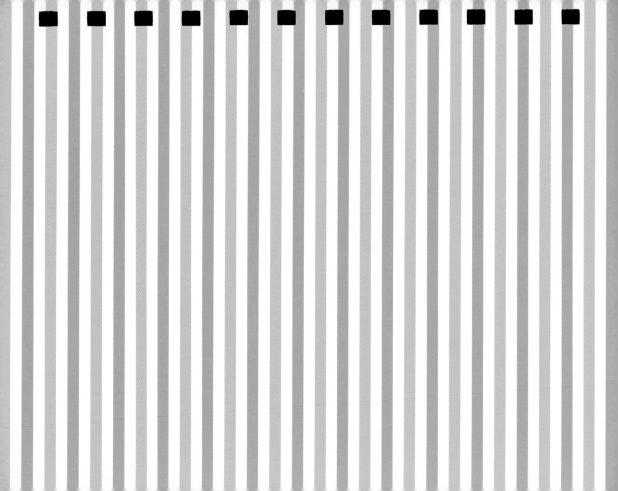

I never made

Who's Who

but I'm featured in

What's That.

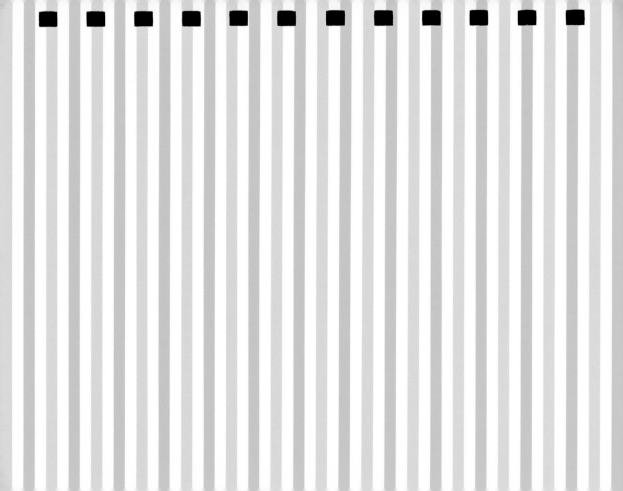

If at first

you do succeed,

try not to look

too astonished.

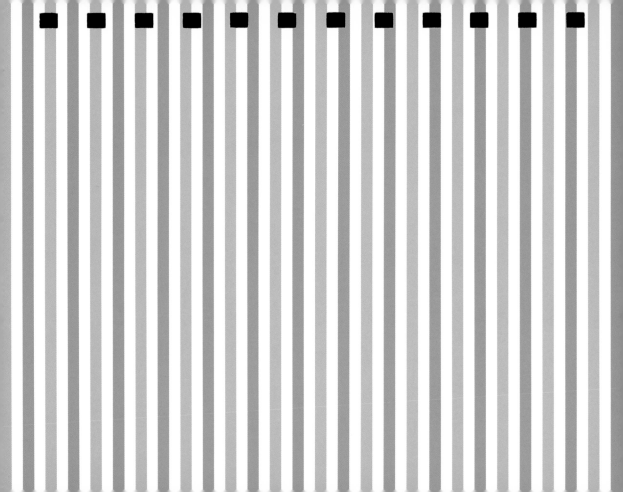

If at first you don't succeed, swallow all evidence that you tried.

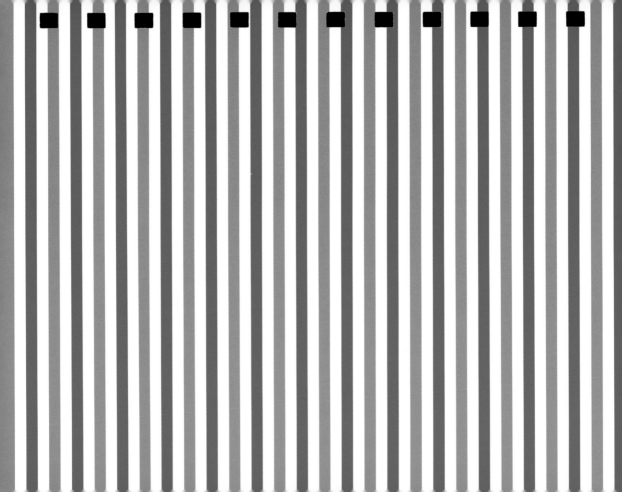

Always take a lawyer with you.

And bring another lawyer

to watch him.

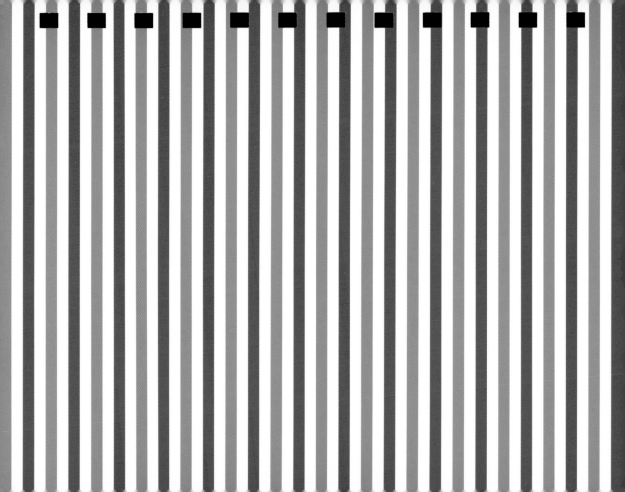

Job placement:

Telling your boss what he

can do with your job.

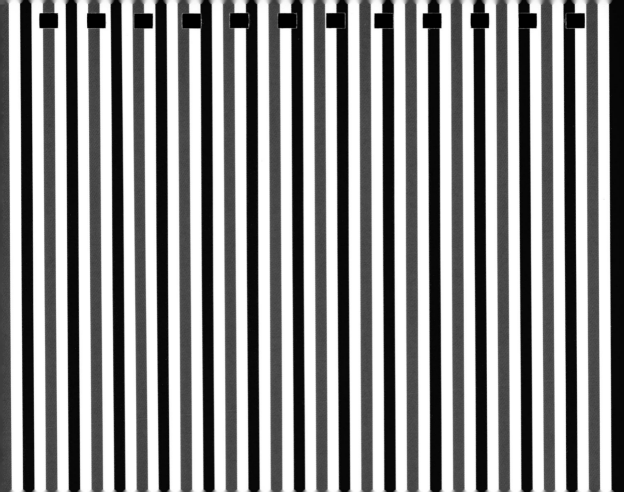

My take-home pay doesn't

even take me home.

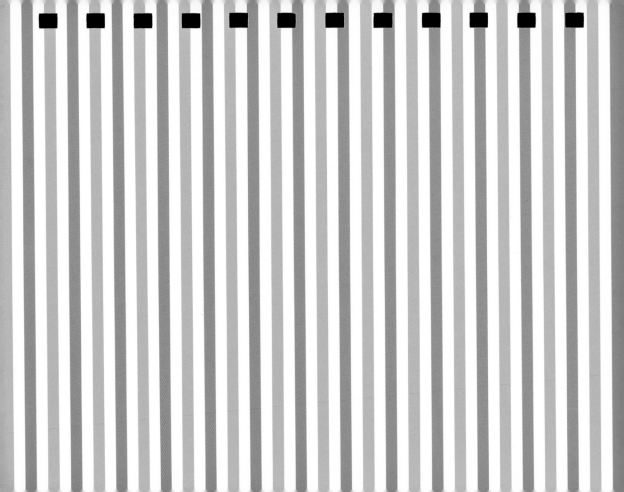

At the end of the money,

I always have some

month left.

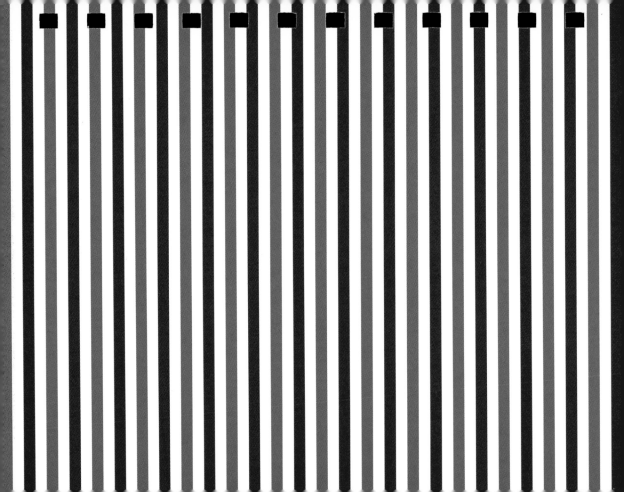

If you can keep your head when all about you are losing theirs —

it's quite possible you haven't grasped the situation.

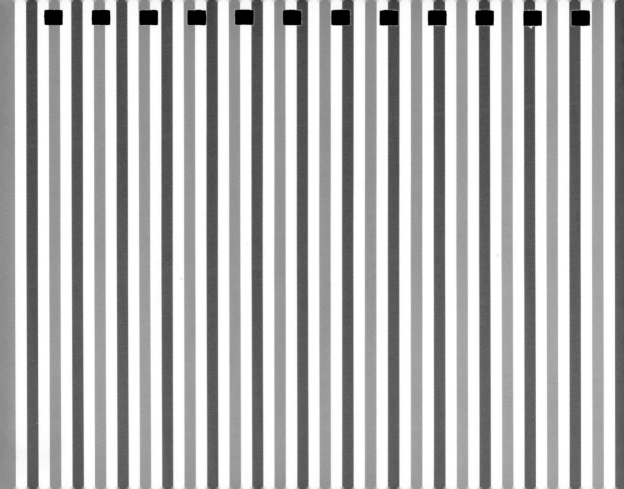

No day is so bad

that it can't be fixed with a nap.

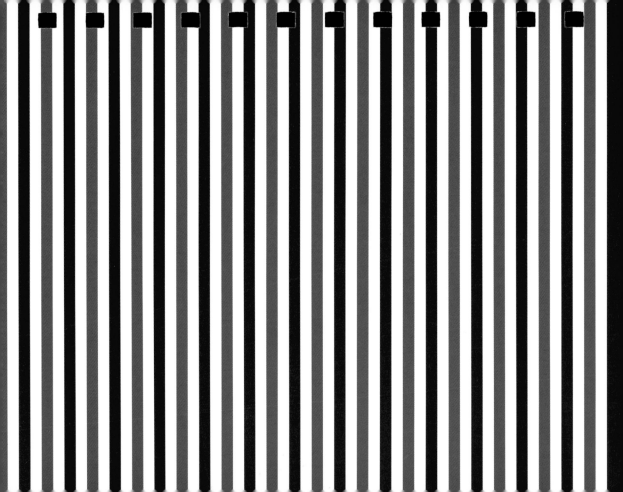

Would you like

to speak to the

man in charge

or the woman

who knows what's

happening?

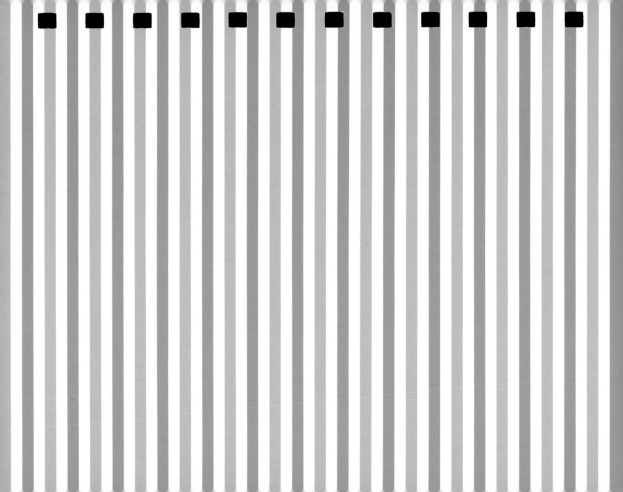

Women like silent men –

they think they're listening.

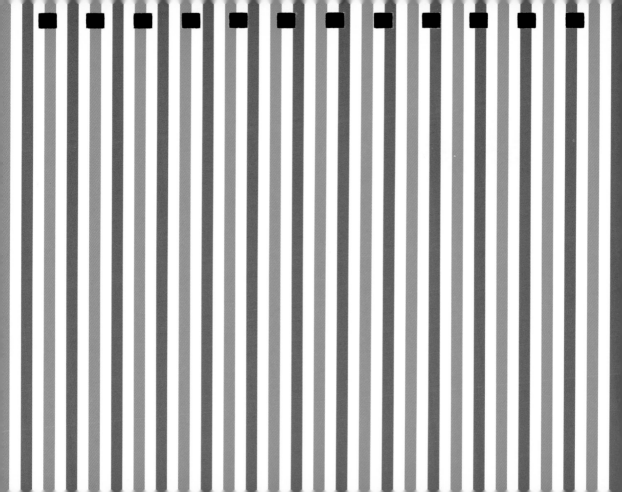

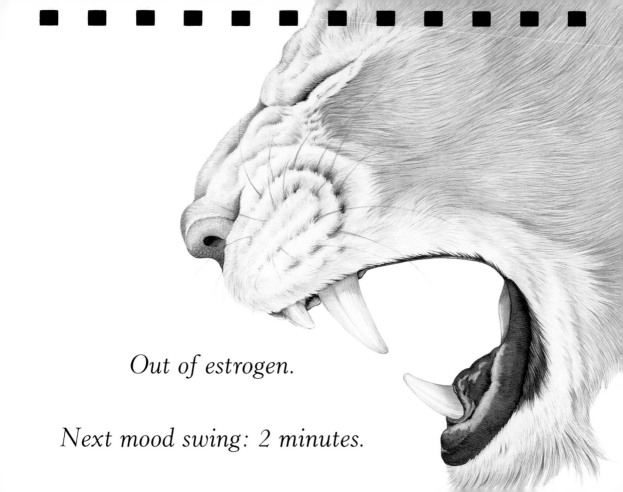

Out of estrogen.

Next mood swing: 2 minutes.

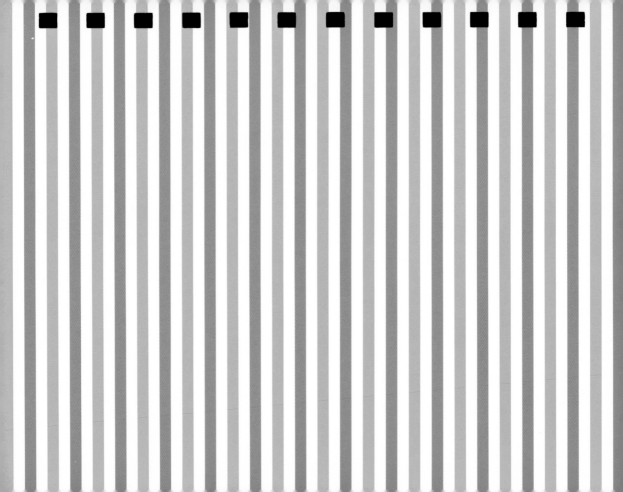

I am **not** tense.

Just terribly, terribly alert.

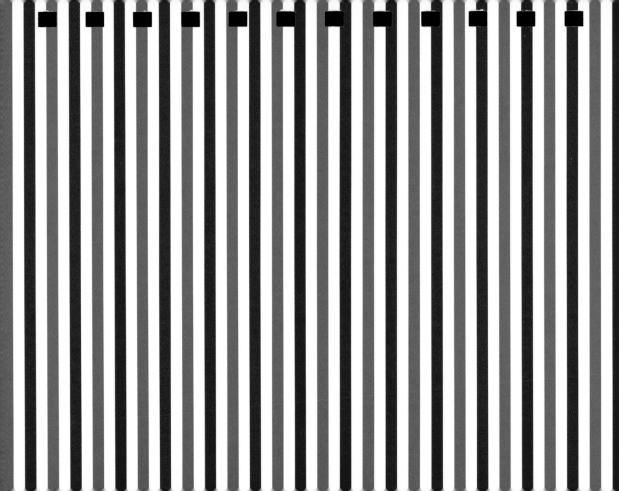

If you don't agree with me,

it means you haven't been listening.

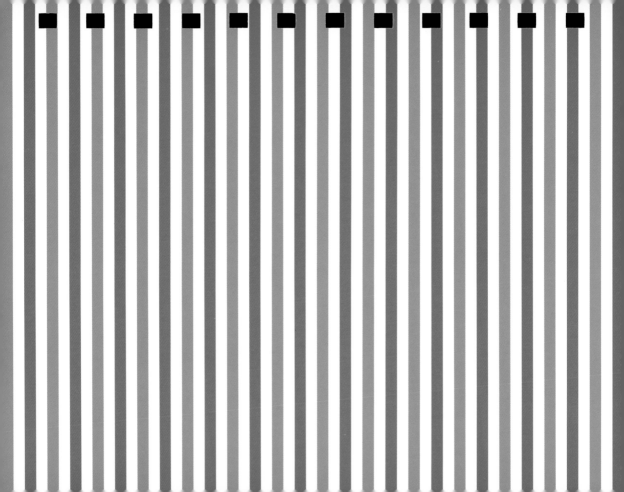

Never go to bed mad –

stay up and fight.

If you

leave me

can I

come too?

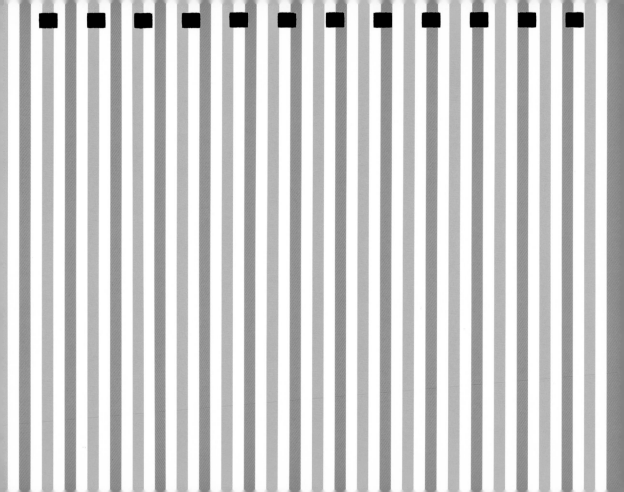

The quickest way for a parent to get a child's attention . . .

is to sit down and look comfortable.

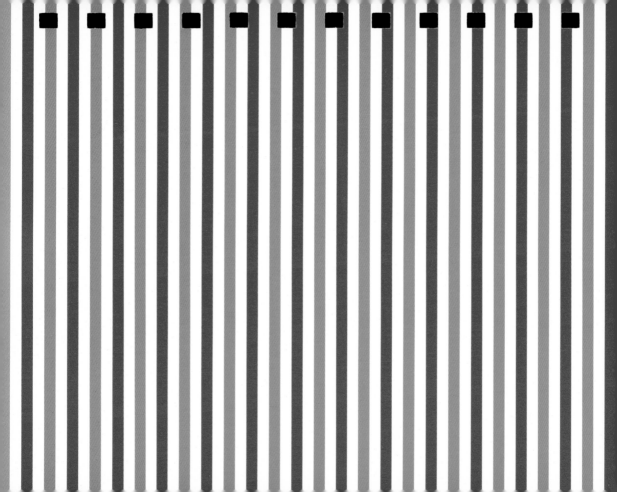

There are few things

more satisfying than seeing

your children have

teenagers of

their own.

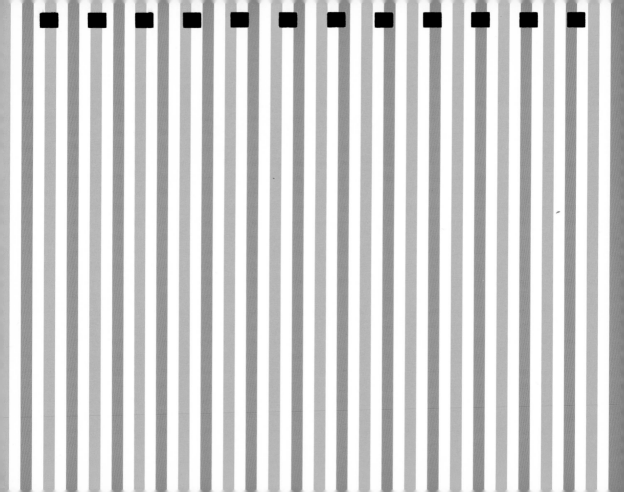

You're only

young once.

That is all society

can stand.

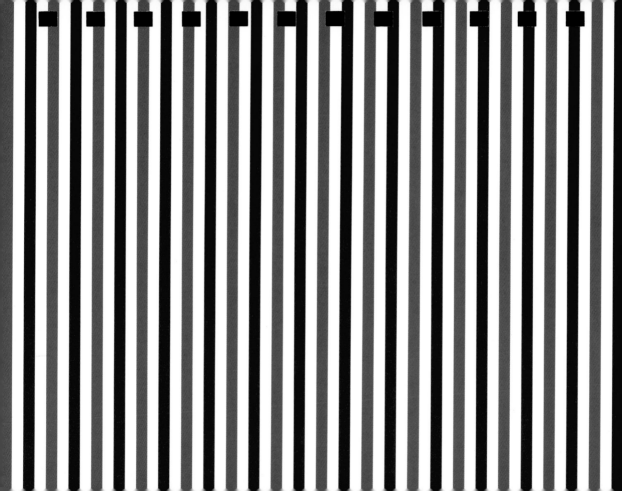

Just let me shop

and no one will get hurt!

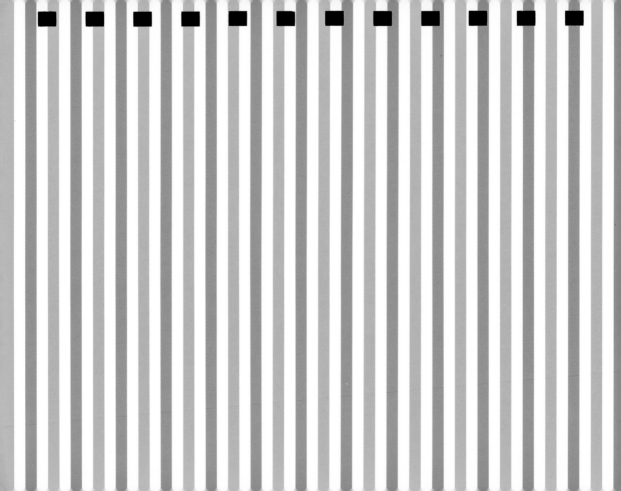

Saw it,

wanted it,

threw a tantrum, *Got It!*

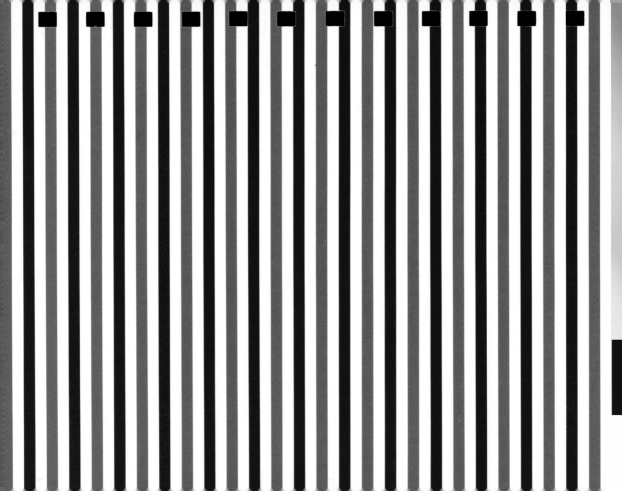

I want it all —

and I want it delivered!

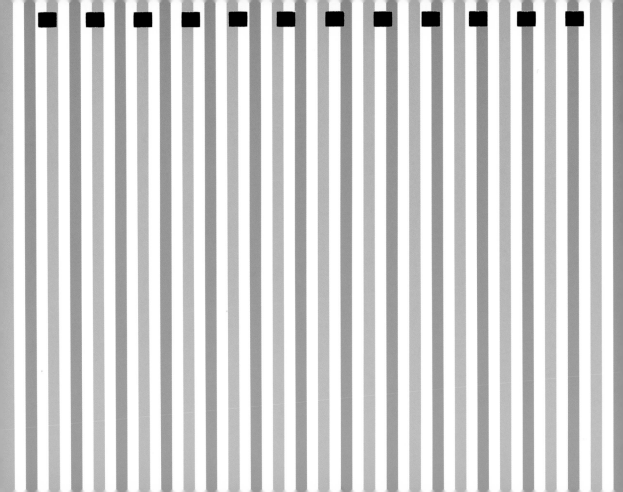

Princess, having had sufficient experience with princes, seeks frog.

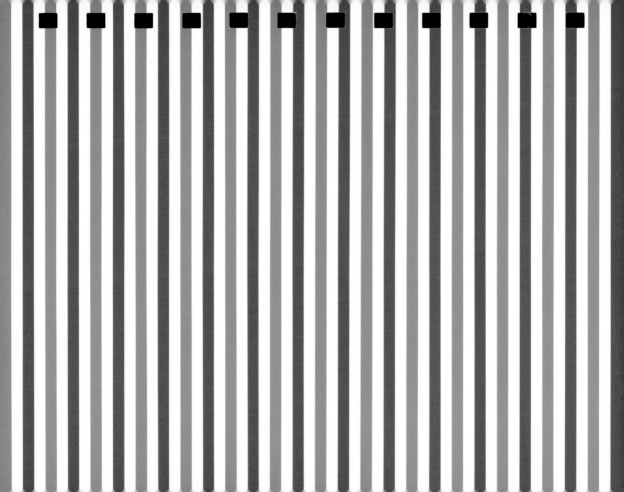

If there's no chocolate

in heaven,

I'm not going.

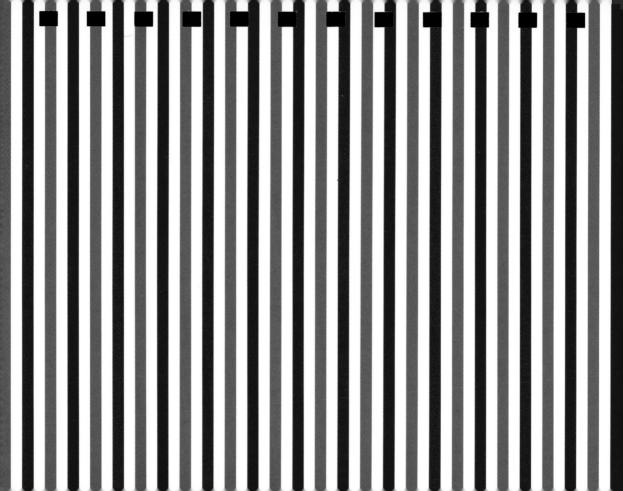

Every time I hear the word "exercise," I wash my mouth out with chocolate.

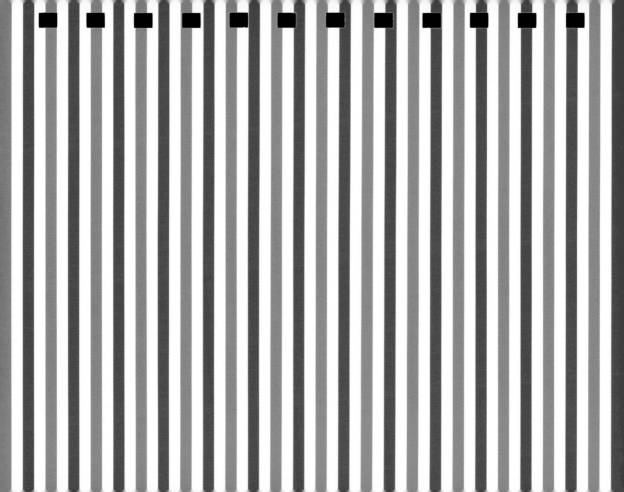

Never eat more

than you can lift.

Too much of a good thing can be wonderful.

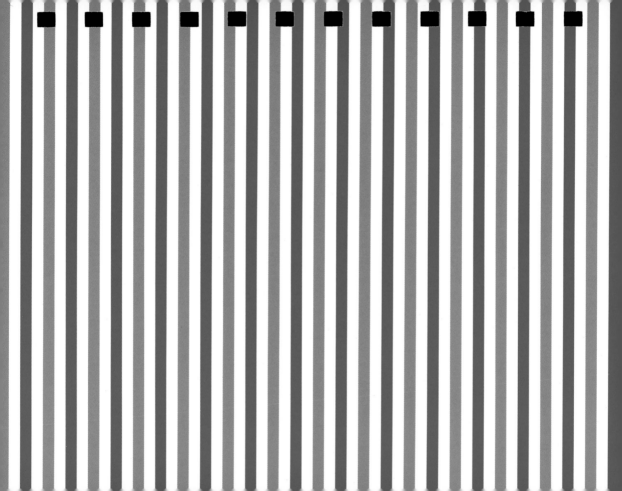

I hate repeating gossip — but really,

what else can you do with it?

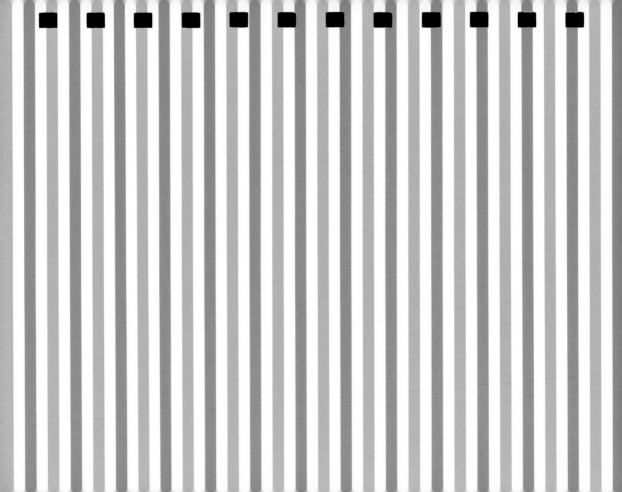

As you get older,
your secrets are
safe with your
friends
because
they can't
remember
them either.

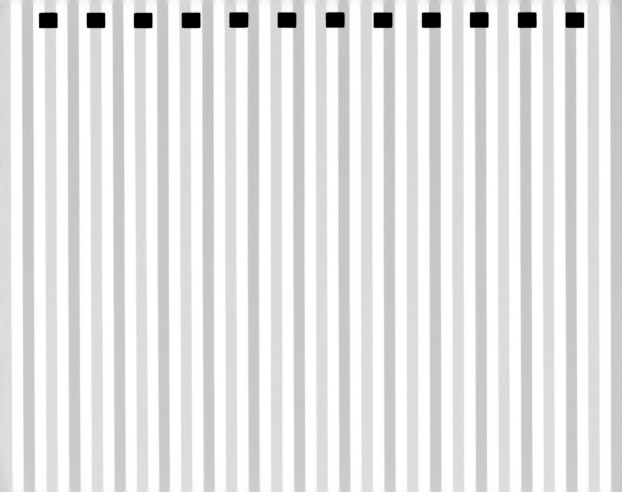

Middle age is when

we can do just

as much as ever

but would rather not.

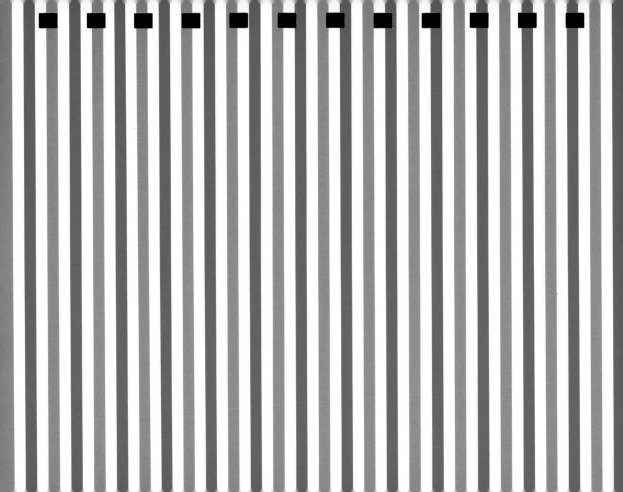

My wild oats

have turned into prunes

and All-Bran.

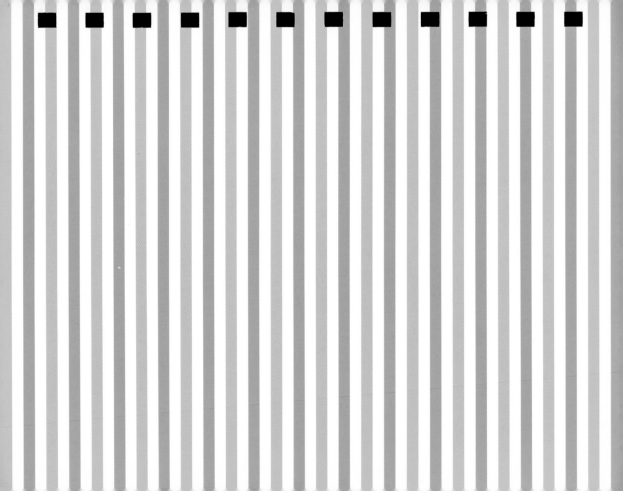

Forget health food.

I'm at an age where I need

all the preservatives

I can get.

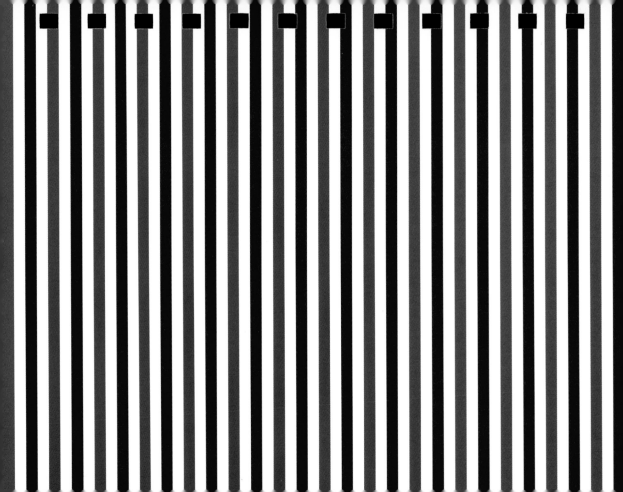

You can't stay

young forever.

But you can be

immature for the

rest of your life.

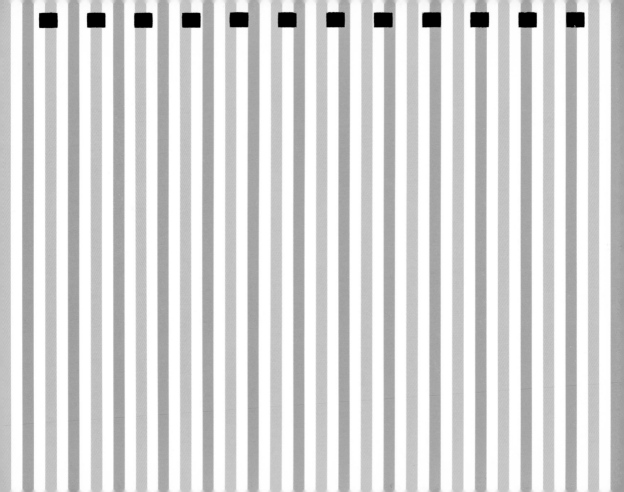

Don't get lost in the shuffle. Shuffle along with the lost.

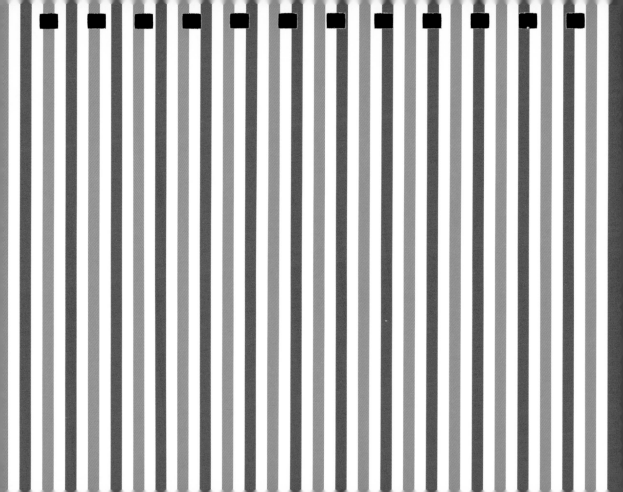

Stay

in

bed —

it's

safer.

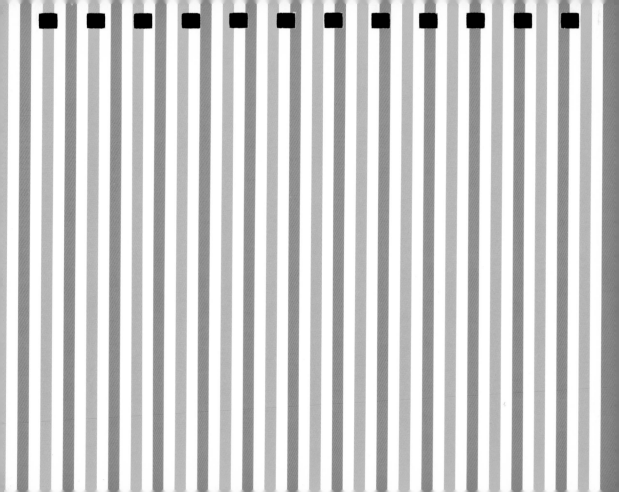

I live in my

own little world.

But it's okay—

they know me here.

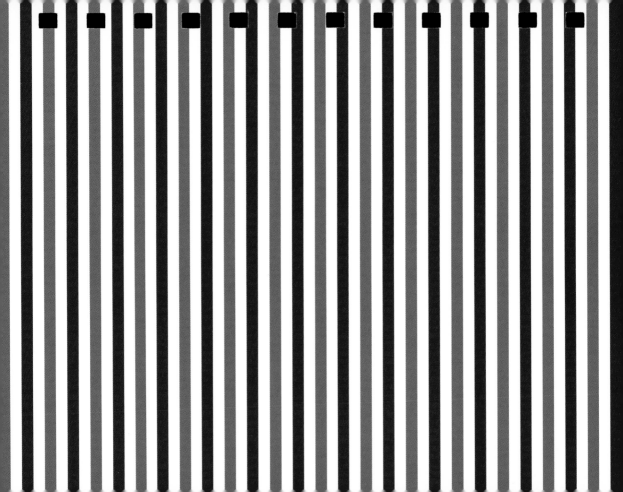

It's been lovely.

But I have to

SCREAM now.

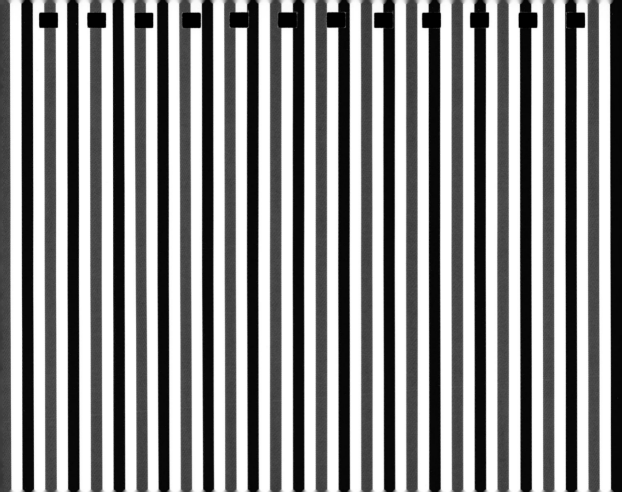

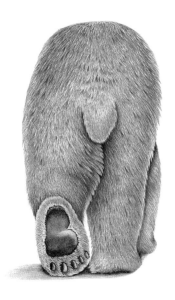

Gone crazy. Back soon.

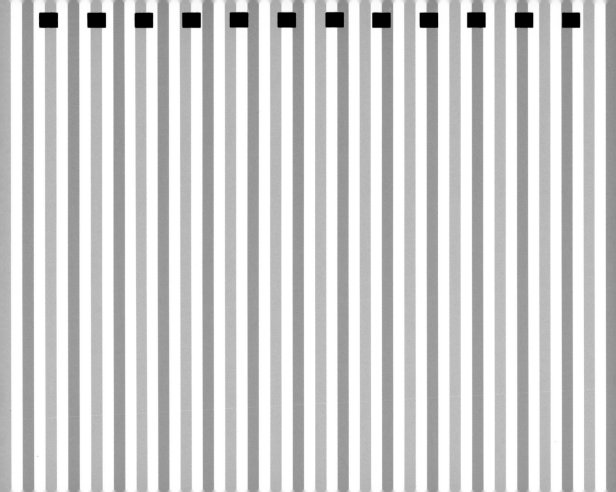

Artist's notes

The art and adages in this collection were chosen from those in the first three *Furry Logic* books. It was great fun for me to pick out my favorites and put them all together in an exciting new format.

All the paintings are watercolor and the finest detail is completed with a tiny sable brush with a single hair at its tip. Unfortunately this all-important hair at the tip wears away too soon and I can go through three or four of these tiny brushes in one painting, especially the bigger paintings. If I am really lucky, one brush will last the entire painting and very occasionally I come across a "super brush" that holds together for two paintings.

All of my original paintings are now available for purchase on the Furry Logic website, www.furrylogicbooks.com, and each painting comes with the sable brush (or brushes!) that was used to complete it.

I hope some of the pages in this collection make you chuckle and that you enjoy the easel format. Please let me know—I always enjoy receiving messages via the website.

Best wishes,

Jane.

www.furrylogicbooks.com

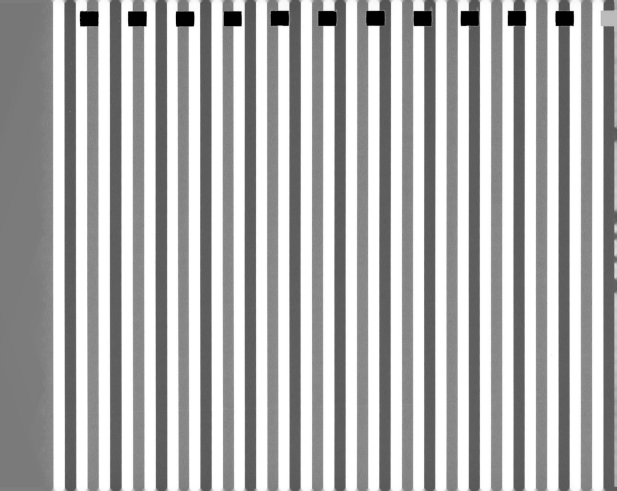

Acknowledgments

Grateful thanks to John Cooney of *Grapevine* magazine, Auckland, New Zealand, for many of the quotations attributed to "Anon." Other quotations appeared or are quoted in the following publications: "Be yourself. Nobody is better qualified." (Anon.) in *More Pocket Positives*, Five Mile Press, Melbourne, Australia. "If at first you do succeed, try not to look too astonished." (Anon.) in *World's Best Humour*, Five Mile Press, Melbourne, Australia. "I never made Who's Who but I'm featured in What's That." (Phyllis Diller) and "You can't stay young forever. But you can be immature for the rest of your life." (Maxine Wilkie) in *Women's Lip*, Sourcebook Inc., Naperville, IL, USA. "If you don't agree with me, it means you haven't been listening." (Sam Markewich) in *Comedy Comes Clean 2*, Three Rivers Press, New York, USA. "If you leave me, can I come too?" (Cynthia Hemmel) and "Middle age is when we can do as much as ever—but would rather not." and "There's no problem so big or complicated that it can't be run away from in." *The Penguin Dictionary of Modern Humorous Quotations*, Penguin Group, London, UK. "I hate repeating gossip—but really, what else can you do with it?" in *The Penguin Dictionary of Jokes*, Penguin Group, London, UK.

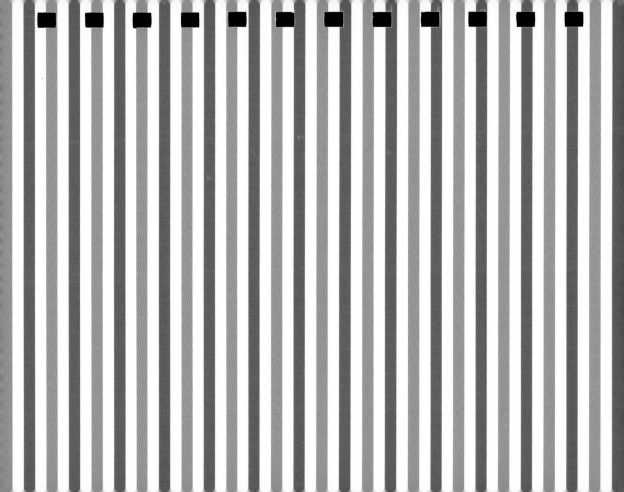

Ten Speed Press

P O Box 7123, Berkeley, California 94707, United States

www.tenspeed.com

Distributed in Canada by Ten Speed Press Canada.

Library of Congress Cataloging-in-Publication Data is on file with the publisher.

ISBN-13: 978-1-58008-836-7
ISBN-10: 1-58008-836-8

Printed in China
First printing, 2006

1 2 3 4 5 6 7 8 9 10— 10 09 08 07 06

For more information visit www.furrylogicbooks.com